Slope of the Child Everlasting

Slope of the Child Everlasting

Poems by
Laurie Kutchins

AMERICAN POETS CONTINUUM SERIES, NO. 103

BOA EDITIONS, LTD.   ROCHESTER, NY   2007

First Edition

Publications and programs by BOA Editions, Ltd.—a not-for-profit corporation under section 501 (c) (3) of the United States Internal Revenue Code—are made possible with the assistance of grants from the Literature Program of the New York State Council on the Arts; the Literature Program of the National Endowment for the Arts; the County of Monroe, NY; the Lannan Foundation for support of the Lannan Translations Selection Series; the Sonia Raiziss Giop Charitable Foundation; the Mary S. Mulligan Charitable Trust; the Rochester Area Community Foundation; the Arts & Cultural Council for Greater Rochester; the Steeple-Jack Fund; the Elizabeth F. Cheney Foundation; Eastman Kodak Company; the Chesonis Family Foundation; the Ames-Amzalak Memorial Trust in memory of Henry Ames, Semon Amzalak and Dan Amzalak; and contributions from many individuals nationwide.

Cover Design: Lisa Mauro
Cover Art: "Scarecrow" by Jeanie Tomanek
Interior Design and Composition: Richard Foerster

BOA Logo: Mirko

Library of Congress Cataloging-in-Publication Data

Kutchins, Laurie.
Slope of the child everlasting : poems / by Laurie Kutchins. — 1st ed.
    p. cm. — (American poets continuum series ; no. 103)
ISBN 978–1–929918–91–1 (pbk. : alk. paper)
1. Children—Poetry. I. Title.

PS3561.U793S58 2007
811'.54–dc22

                                    2006030253

BOA Editions, Ltd.
Nora A. Jones, Executive Director/Publisher
Thom Ward, Editor/Production
Peter Conners, Editor/Marketing
Glenn William, BOA Board Chair
A. Poulin, Jr., President & Founder (1938–1996)
260 East Avenue, Rochester, NY 14604
www.boaeditions.org

for Helen, among the sages

> *The descent beckons*
> *as the ascent beckoned.*
> *Memory is a kind*
> *of accomplishment,*
> *a sort of renewal*
> *even*
> *an initiation...*

"The Descent"
William Carlos Williams

Contents

Slope of the Child Everlasting

Togwotee

Atop this white divide be still, be the horned owl after hunger.
Marry my little ear to a stone in the wind's two-ocean river.

Churn me open, spawn of death, spine of summer thunder.
Bring mud and hummingbird back to rock, cloud, river.

Then teach me winter. Let me learn leaving and returning are the same
Yearning of breath: *you can go anywhere from here* murmurs upriver.

Remember mother-of-pearl, father wading out to fish the sandbar.
Remember silt and eggs, the child of clay, the slope below the river.

Let mouth be our meeting, brother to the ocean's inland quiver,
Sister into snow driven seven directions down river.

Song of the Turtle Unburrowing

Was it the sweet smell
of the thalia daffodil
that woke me,

the ruckus of the garden lunging
back into the world,
was it the urge
of the bloodroot?

Under leaf-mold,
under old grass cuttings
beside the southern
brick of a house

my blunt red eyes
have opened.

Not the bright smiling red
of cardinals flashing
in the leafing woods

not the redbud red—
double doses of beauty—
not me.

I was always the earth's
brown-red, almost
bereft green,

always the stone's
circular endurance.
Am I loved?

I dreamed all winter
I lived inside the soft
red cup of the tulip.

I was alchemical
without shell,

my shadow so gold
it could blind.
But look,

I still come back
like rock
caked with mud.

Deep in the subtle
mulch I risk
the spring wind

teasing my beak
as if it wished
I were the robin

flittering to remake
the nest in the mock
orange shade
I'll summer under.

If I had song
nimble enough
for the sky
how quick

the mockingbird
would lift it,
my earthborn music

how quick
it would fall and
burrow back.

Skin

Everything has a voice, even the skin
the black snake left beside the house
the day the golden tulips bloomed
and overpowered the sun. Never seen,
that snake leaves its skin behind
each spring like a secret gift
no longer dark or urgent without
its body. *Oh*
look at me, I've grown
and grown more beautiful, its voice
thralls from the grass, all
its language new and moving
in the skin like thunder
gathering into a noon
yet to form:
Have you heard me
down in the ductwork
of your house
living on mice?
Have you lived yet
a day without fear?
If not skin, what
will you come to shed?

April Nights

Moon, like a husk of corn in the making.

It's empty again, small farmhouse across the road.
The white clapboard glowing its own.

Wide-eyed and croupy at four A.M., outside in my arms,
my toddler who is learning to talk stops coughing,
notices over us the whisker of moon
and wheezes, "where's grandpa?"

These nights in the country,
once the dogs are quiet: so much silence

and then a whole question,
a car making the curve

or a blouse of wind sounding like the sigh
of someone pulling through a coma,
at last the other side.

And the moon again. Husk in the making.

The Voice Outside

What was it
the voice said to no one
a few moments ago?
I was walking across the grass
crossing from shed to house,
I was going
to write it down.

It's April
and I was impatient
for the turtle
to come forth.

I was brushing aside
an urge to pull
the layers off,
October grass and leaves
I'd piled over her,

bring the noon sun down
to her dull shell,
wake her

as if she were a sleeping baby
before she was ready
to crawl from beneath
all her own.

The livid hiss
of another wild turtle
I plucked and saved
from the hill road

that unreasonably warm
week in January was still
with me.

I almost mistook it
for a stone.

Untimely neck bloodied
from ruptures
on both sides
of its thumbed head,
his red eyes pussed
under my hands.

I was only to guess
at what danger: teeth,
talons, or determined
beak of a raptor.

It is good to inhabit a myth
without knowing
all of it.

The turtle is the truest
Persephone,
going under half the year.

Was it
come back to me,
the voice whispering
vowels at noon
to no one?

I was crossing,
I was going to stop
below the black window

and peer down,

and then up,
as close to the crouched gods
as I could get
reaching
toward the light.

Whisper

Don't look back. I thought I heard the river
whisper early one morning.

Or was it a child's voice drifting and rising
from the current and waiting

all these years for someone
such as me to pass?

If the whisper was the river,
I'd have nothing to do with its voice

but walk and listen.
The river's one direction is forward

for the ocean, for evaporation,
so why should the river need to look back?

It already knows it will transmute
and fall down to itself.

But if the whisper was a child
I would have to go in

and stand in its icy paradox.
I'd have to hear it

and not listen.
Go under and

look back hard.

River Keeper

How clear the river is
only moments after loss.

Gurgle of a sandhill crane.
Orange flash of a western tanager.

Sagebrush that needs the rain.
I found a simple bench carved from an evergreen.

A plaque in stone with a boy's name,
two dates that subtract

to nineteen years.
River, do you know him?

Someone is building a new bridge across
without handrails.

When I walk on it I get dizzy
from wanting to hold on.

Under there's the long young spine.
Always the swift current,

never the same. And the river,
more stones than stars.

Poppies

Impatient for beauty I assumed
they were only weeds
and pulled them from the untended bed
I should have known
anything to leave the ground
so willingly
would impart the worth of waiting
forgive me
I dismissed the chipped rock owl looking on
aghast the broken angel
embedded on her granite back
I ignored the true weeds the musk
of the flowerless lemongrass
overgrown grapevine invasive rose of Sharon
glaring gardeners who came before me
to the circle of stones
give me a second chance
to watch the hairy gonad bud sacs
spiked leaves strong drooping necks
quiver and break coral skirts
black seeds
no summer wind scatters
beneath to become the frightful bloom
my head is drooped my roots threatened
my feral recital please
I am just learning to know flowers
I have always known only rock and stone
a safer thing

The First Time I Saw My Father Cry

He was the age I am now.
We had already driven two days
east across the dry high grasses
of the Great Plains, crossed
the Missouri, the corn farms,
his mountains blue resolve
in the rearview.
He was taking me to college.
I was terribly unprepared.
From the car I studied
the heartland quilted into flat
stinking farms. Silos rising,
gray trees I had no names for.
Water towers bearing the names
of Minnesota towns.
He bought me a nice dinner,
a wool dress coat to block
the cold. He hauled up dorm
steps the clunky orange bicycle,
typewriter, my mother's
transatlantic trunk.
When there was nothing left of me
in his car I walked him
out where he'd parked,
a dirt drive tunneled by lilacs
shriveling with late summer.
He hesitated
and loomed, keys clenched
in hand, eyes made bigger
and bluer by the sudden
form of tears. All granite gone.
He became a stranger

pliant and weepy, from whom I hurried
down the lane that
nine months later would bloom
and perfume
the college and the town, antidote
to the shit heaped
over every new crop,
to find him
as I had not known.

Last Gift

My father was excited. He waited for a family gathering to
give us his gift, the quarter-century of slides he'd compressed
and assembled into a half-hour video. We closed draperies

in the den, sipped on flutes of champagne as he pressed
the play button. He hadn't known he could add sound. We
staggered back to a silent family there in the TV screen,

three grainy children lined up with no voices, well-clothed,
inert, poised as little windbreaks beside the house and stiffened
into like smiles, shallow crypts of lips and eyes unable to hide

grim tedium, fear, a mean creature scowling inside my older sister,
my younger brother's frenetic cowlick the beginning of the alcoholic,
my good angel vacancies. Generous and spare, at times I glimpsed

light shining through. How could I not thank him for that gift,
his last to remind us we'd come of age under the stern eye
of the brown box camera, its leather strap tight across his chest.

I watched another family unearth itself in the viewing,
brush a rock-chalk powder across our grown up faces, twist
its sadness into the room like an old family ghost

no one willingly sees, let alone speaks to. Later, in privacy,
my husband spoke of it. And to it. He reached across that chasm,
touched where my wings were and said *I see you now.*

Clothesline

Like my mother always did I hold the spare clothespins three
at a time in my mouth. I know this as silence, my mouth
not a voice but a basket. She did it well, clipped the
family's clothes close and taut, maintained the line
between clean and secret dirt from wash to wash,
ankles to shoulders flapping from wire. She
never understood the wind but trusted it
to whip the wash stiff and ready for
the steamy hiss of an iron under
an hour of sunlight.
Silent time.

All winter the crows in the disheveled elms of yet another rental
house haunt the limbs above the clothesline. I do not know
why they winter in these trees, there's no food for them here,
why they keep screeching above our clothes, our dull
bedding. I've adjusted to their raucous music,
their pasty droppings that sometimes appear like
berry stains darkening our clean, wind-
fragrant wash.

My son's clothes are getting so big yet he outgrows them faster
than they wear. Soon his favorite orange turtleneck with paint
stains on the sleeves will no longer fit, he will not be
able to snap the jeans fraying in the knee where a granule
of gravel has lived a dark speck beneath his skin since
he was three. I've given up on his socks that
keep the permanent grit of playground
sand through the hearty
wash cycle.

My husband's flung shirts with their lost buttons take up so much
space on the line, flannel sleeves that have drawn me into the
smells of fresh paint and sawdust, the lovely energy
of his arms, the haphazard blousiness of boxers.
He's survived so many accidents, a live wire
scrambled his heart, burned holes through
his socks and work boots, killed our friend.
He never uses clothespins, there is so
little tidiness in his domesticity,
so little time how incredible
he's alive.

My father's T-shirts were embarrassing and thin to me, how
shapeless the worn cotton stretched into holes the wind
muscled through on the line. I don't think he ever
regretted how hard he worked through his childhood
and mine, he never called it unhappiness because
he saw it as frugal necessity. He liked his legs in
patched denims, when a sleeve was torn
he cut it down to a shorter sleeve, he
loved rags.

Mom took such care to dress well, she had a beautiful body, she
sunbathed and sipped iced coffee and read a book while
waiting for the clothes to dry on the line, she bought
my older sister and me matching outfits which
meant I wore the same thing double the years,
first the fresh and costly garments twinned
with sister, then the hand-me-downs
drab and limp against my
shy skin.

Dad talked so little of his beginnings, every story mattered.
He told me his widowed mother took in laundry to make
ends meet. Mondays were washdays for her own six
children. She kept the iron hot Tuesdays through

Thursdays, washdays for money. Fridays were
to clean house, Saturdays for cooking, baking
and bathing. Sundays were Bibles, sermons
and rest to get ready for Mondays to
begin again.

That family rarely speaks of Selma, the youngest, after she was
strangled by her new husband and folded into a refrigerator.
She'd met him through a national Christian classifieds,
so happy they found each other not through looks
but prayers answered, and fell in love through
letters and then phone calls for a whole
year before they met and
quickly married.

Bedroom Beside a Field

Some nights we sleep without touching.
Some nights entwined like grapes
in the arbor up the road. Some nights
I wake to the twists of the baby
in her crib across the hall,
the boy downstairs blowing his nose
or taking a dark suck of water.
In this room I often dream
I can't find my way home.

Late summer in the thrash
of dark mornings, a whippoorwill
bids me to the window.
I search the field beneath our bedroom,
waft of ragweed, barn cats
and uncut grasses.
It is a hollow call, the sound
of a ghost-child I've never seen.

We sleep above a box turtle
that survives on crickets
in the tall grass and burrows close
beside the house when nights rehearse
the first frost. We sleep under eaves
where yellow jackets knit their
papery gray nests to survive
the seasons of ice.

My belly swelled with last child in this room.
I woke to labor in a snowstorm,
our neighbor pacing the field
the night his father died.

In all hours of the moon I've rocked
an infant's hunger, a baby's teething,
colic and descent.

Beyond the bedroom where the field ends
there is a tall black locust. Half scorched
and rotted, struck by lightning
just after we moved in,
it rises three times the height
of all the other trees.

Are you God, or some god? I often look up
and ask, but get no answer.
I sense he beds down in the high thin limbs
of that locust tree but I cannot prove it
since he has never cried out or
woken me like the whippoorwill
or made a sound
like crickets or rain, children
or a man
on his ribside sleeping.

Old Man's Song for the Coming of Fall

Don't make me lie down in a hammock—
let the rest of the world go hang

I don't want to rock back and forth
like a baby again

napping in the gnarled shade
of the orchard I nursed and raised

until my trees outgrew me
I want to work again

harvest the apple and the peach
climb the ladder fill the crates

a boy whistles summer his whole life
but I hear the cold sod calling

I want to mow the meadow back
disk the corn paint the fence

reach the highest roses
on the arbor ladder

my heart in its north wind
trembling

red flare where hummingbirds gather
while the world hangs on

I am homesick to go
time to squish time open

slurp its juice suck
the hard pit and go

September Fever

Not even noon and the small girl
        who never stops chattering has fallen
asleep under the brown Guatemalan
        blanket. She doesn't remember
the night, how she cried out restless
        with fever and thunder.
Lightning lit up her whole body
        with shivers,
rain, then something harder
        lashed the metal roof,
clanked the chimney flue.
        In one night wind out of the north
shoved aside the whole
        fat hayroll of summer.

All morning the clouds churn
        over the mountains, unsettled
as the red-tailed hawks screeching
        grace over the chasm.
First snow drains the green
        out of each aspen heart.
The cabin logs crack and shrink
        from the sudden change,
the child's tummy, forehead, back
        flushed and exhausted, trying to hold
the heat of summer an hour longer.
        How like another husk
she wilts and flares.

Child's Song for the End of Summer

green box turtle I lost you happy
yellow kite I let go and gone

red swing mine the shedding pines
grass drooping to kiss the dust of August

I have two hearts   I'll give you one
I have more eyes   take mine

one two three whippoorwill
where are you hiding

one two three crickets
why are you black and shining

day you make a fluffed brown tail
night you make a sore throat

with your voice in my ears
with your voice in my ears

fall trembles me
fall trembles me

summer you are
thrumming slower

why for why for

Mountain Train

Two boys dash to stand on whichever side
   Two old men hoe their thin alpine garden and
rides the most dangerous ledge of cliff
   no longer look up when the train rocks past
up up the long steep mountain. They shift
   early each morning and late each afternoon.
back and forth from one side to the other,
   One feels lucky to have lost only a knuckle
leaning and waving the long slope down,
   in the war. In the other, every other tooth
fingers curled atop the open windows,
   is gold or gone. They hardly speak but work
leaving smudges of chips and sweets.
   side by side, resting in the mountain shadow.
Wind born in a canyon musses their hair.
   When did they stop talking? When

They chatter, rock and chatter as the train
   did they stop waving back to those boys?
clanks, rocks up and hours after back
   Sparse and floating: the tartness of lemon drops,
down the mountain. In the mathematical
   hallways that smelled of the opulence of uncles,
logic of the child, they make noise to prove
   the meticulous ticking of wall clocks.
they exist. They must. To be silent
   A whole life in that apparent back and forth.
is to be invisible, to not have happened.
   In which something happened.

Mount Zion Road

Nameless, this road was just a number when I moved here. County
    Road 752,
upslope past 721's right angle turn to the Glen, past the white fence
    bridge
over Joe's Creek, the immaculate garden of Ruby Dove and her
    daughter,
past the curved road over Green Hill where we often swerve to miss
    deer,
dead possum, skunk, fox squirrels, field cats, turtles, bottles of beer,
Calvin Sheets's house and peacock aviary perched at the wooded crest.

They named the roads a few years back for the sake of county 911 calls.
I was away when they drilled new signs with local names: Well Hollow,
Glen Hollow, Frog Hollow, Joe's Creek, Milk Creek, Dove's Lane,
Green Hill, Grist Mill, Hollar School, Fox Squirrel, Whippoorwill.
Biblical and unlocal, Mount Zion is the misfit.
I live on this road where my heart won't settle.

Up the north hill knoll is its namesake, Mt. Zion Church of the
    Brethren.
A rural post-confederate church white with tall green shutters,
a large cross bolted to one side of the double doors. I walk past
but have never entered, the doors locked the six days aside from
Sundays. When I peer through a keyhole I see more green:
mosaics of Jesus intact in glassy plastic.

Across the road white and black Holsteins wander the hillsides
grazing. A gray clapboard barn and a silo. Farms and cropland
form the rippled folds of the valley and beyond, the farthest line
I can see from where I stand on the church knoll,
the mossy, prehistoric spine of Massanutten Mountain.
It's pastoral ground twice burned by General Sherman.

Who are the Brethren? In the church cemetery I sometimes
wander with the baby. She likes an old child's stone. It's small
with an engraved lamb and words she can't yet read, *daughter*,
and *oh precious sleep*. When the stone burns warm from the sun
she rests on an unnamed grief long gone and sucks her thumb.
Its only flowers are those blown loose from the other headstones.

I find the same names in the cemetery as on the mailboxes all up and
  down
Mount Zion Road. Not one lives in my veins. A neighbor brings me
  tracts
on Jews as unenlightened Christians: he believes it is just a matter of
  time.
I wonder which families may have Native or African blood. Would they
know? Would it unsettle their proud names? Though I often walk
  among
their bones and names, the dead along my road don't know me.

Once, I found my grandfather's grave in an abandoned Jewish cemetery
that survived outside of Freiburg, Germany. I felt lucky to find the stone
with his name. Lucky he died before becoming a number. I've nothing
of his to pass on to a great-granddaughter except December, a morning
with hoarfrost laced across his star, long before I came to a road named
Mount Zion, in a place that keeps certain histories burning in silence.

The Light We Winter Under

December again. All year a dry weeping took up residence—a corridor,
a dim boarding house, rooms with small white sinks where a girl lived
until she could not. I came to womanhood not feeling a thing.

Like a strong dream, winter light is the fiercest of the year.
It arrives late and after everything, it disappears
as it wakes you.

A letter put off for years gets hastily written
and sent within an afternoon.
It's that kind of light.

On the plaza the Andean men sell woolen caps, mittens
and one-size-fits-all sweaters. Our blunt sun warms the wool,
giving the whole afternoon an animal smell.

I turned the wall calendar to its last page—
a watercolor done by a child sent to Terezin, the stopover art camp
before Auschwitz, no date, no signature.

It happens fast, the sailboat drifting from dark to light in the child's
    picture.
Hard to tell if it's fire or water, a flame or a tear in the foreground.
What's forming on the other side not yet finished.

Late afternoon, the clouds build flat, western cities.
The sun retreats in them, hidden and southern.
Now the buildings shine with a dark and wordless purpose.

He says, "I've begun to listen for the sound of the train every night."
She, "There will be no more children."

In the fancy restaurant on the top floor all eyes turn
to the elderly couple slow dancing between courses.

Is it only the long-married and the newly in-love who take
such time, turning everyday chatter and dinner into joy?

December again. The crowd stood and waited a long while
in the line to post their letters.

The self to the self must interrogate tenderly under the light we
winter under.
Do you remember crying because you had no language,
because it could not mother you? Does an infant weep?

Can we live inside the dark memory of the body to that long ago?
Sounds of wheels and stairs, wind under the milkbox,
that was you, weeping.

He says, "We have no directions to the party."
She, "Now I can say I am in love with you."

Wind of My Childhood in the Night

It sounded like a lost dry ocean
erosion unchecked
the milkbox groaned
on the side step
the refinery steamed
and stank
the midnight whistle blew
dark was more than dark
tables chairs overturned dishes
shattered a door slammed
on its hinge and mother
wilted into her gown
wind sounded like
sobbing

deep under the sucked-out blankie
I was blanking
birds in my chest
a dead dog's head
decapitated sacrifices
for staying
good and silent

it sounded like loose clapboard
ripped shutters slapped
to the ground metal trashcans
clattered in the road
morning would come and
my little brother pack
his rucksack and walk
out to the edge of
the world again

wind would boom push
and return
velocities of sleeves
slurry in the pipelines
tumbleweeds clotting
the rigged barbed wire fencing
deep down beneath the crust
I knew that fossils
safe in their beds
were waking
and shattering under drills.

Under the Risings

All my life you have been trying to come back to me with your
white map.
Carry me through this whiteout, the white whispering *you must not
lose the baby,*
whispering, *poppyseeds come from the other world, under the risings of
sweet bread.*
My father's forehead has a boyhood scar, wind broke through a
window: fossil
of the old man who still pedals windward and uphill on his bicycle.
Please kiss the calloused hands of all who allow magic into the cold
shed.

Nests pushed down, the grackles shriek along the oak slats of the
skeletal shed.
Oh hush and say you love me. Let your fingers wander my pregnant
map.
In the tall ditch grass, air whistles through the spokes of a dropped
bicycle.
Each spring under the wild white dogwood a woman lies down
beside her baby.
How old are you, how many betrayals are embedded in us as fossils
and kitchen smells: salt flecks, sesame skins, mother's dark
unleavened bread.

Keep this secret, and I'll hum to you while yeast beads the
beginnings of bread.
Surely you'd be happy among rocks, working at play in a paradoxical
shed.
I'll find you a shovel in the dirt cellar, let you reshape the white fossil
bluffs. Not every river can be found on the classroom pull-down map.
Not everyone grates glass, occupies an egg, plays in a cupboard like
a baby.

Full of red mud and madness the river swifts down river. Sacrifice
the bicycle.

You walk on one side, me on the other, holding the handlebars of a
bicycle.
Between us, a river with hills rising into gold loaves of bread.
Everything else must happen in the snatched silences of the sleeping
baby,
the milk snake laying eggs in the woodpile beside the tool shed,
the sand dunes and stars rippling all night into a lost ship's map,
the child tracing the whole animal pattern from fossils.

Erosion is the bloodhound's name. It sniffs out shallow cribs of fossils,
follows riverbeds junked with wheels, fender chrome from old bicycles.
A thousand broken sleeps have brought us to this place beyond the map
where your mute body becomes my tongue and tastes ceremonial
bread.
The first time you knocked and entered, I told you to leave my shed,
go back to your cavern. I was startled and afraid you'd take my baby.

I've seen your ancient face come back in the face of an hour-old baby,
but then you're gone. In shale beds I once found you in a round
whole fossil
my shovel could not budge, in a caldera shining like skin the earth shed.
Smells of manure, field-thaw, and sawdust float among the soft
bicycled
hills. Nor does dusk last. This is another moon braiding its bread
within our bodies. Once entwined, we'll hold no trace, no map.

Once entwined, we will map your fontanel inside the fossil.
Restore the bicycle, redeem your lost voice from the failed bread.
Dwarfed, old though you are, I know you as the baby I cannot shed.

Song for the Coming of Winter

Snowprints on the cold sidewalk.
           Let that old man go.

Pot roast and potatoes in the kitchen.
           Let him tantrum and collapse.

Neither blizzard nor tumor has him.
           Let him sleep across his supper.

So the bean pot boils over more than once.
           Let him demand of you ten hands.

Here comes the night wind across the hearth.
           Let him dissolve into it.

Neither moon nor shovel has him.
           Let him form again.

Here comes the drop before storm.
           Let that baby go.

A Visit with Jackson Pollock in January

I.

Double espressos to go   wet snow falling
sidewalk ice   guttural slush   lost   you made these lines
creep around the corners of a long Manhattan block

men in trench coats and caps
          women in clogs and black cloqué hats
umbrella splotches soak the MoMA's parquet foyer floor

don't slip behind the exhibition door
don't shiver under your muddle
my baby's captivated by your meticulous messes   your stained thumbs

my boy eyes the wall sideways measuring the paint's thick grip
dividing technique from intensity he's not seen on a wall
a boy fathoms
          being stung equally by light and dark
          kinesis overdose for one floor of an afternoon.

II.

This is a dark month: I hear your voice in the unsettled paint.
Take a ticket for a senior citizen   walk with us
let me take your arm
                         offer a wedge of orange

     won't you play being eighty-seven

look through a baby's eyes
                         tilt your head like a boy?

I want to hear the whole music
        the thin spinning sound of wind's other colors
                across the wide canvas

your cry a wet mop of vodka slapping your noons
        your tangos in sand
              your jazz.

Retina of the Absaroka
        white spine dividing east from west
    finale of the desolate brush
      we sense the inexhaustible
        in whatever we survive.

The loops of memory
      are not the same as the word *wind*
        on the page
its soft gummed bite
      spring's blink and then the blur
        of summer

    tell me what you remember:

III.

months are mops and dark dribbles a purge under blur
and nudges east a finale of slaps and wet night a
blink with vodka twigs a fathom of captives
sugar and jazz

shivers of orange and ice a brilliance of thumbs
afternoons a wedge into the wide page of mouths
diddles with drips west and loops a tango of
slush and arteries

doors a baby's flood in a hat a snowfall of eyes dividing
slips from soft messes places with spines grips in blocks
and wind a wash of sand kinesis tilted arc of
play and light

muddles equal under shadows and floors a retina of canvas
and unsettled summer overdose remember music you sense
block and clog

Waking

1.

To find myself surrounded
by a huddle of scientists. Tell us,
their stern foreheads pressed close,
tell us how to describe the anatomy
of the imagi...

2.

To the sound of rain falling
in a desert where rain is prayer.
A small child touched my throat
to ask what happens
to men's eyes when they die.

3.

Because of an unreliable alarm and a ringing phone.
Three embryos float out
in a little boat:
Winkin, Blinkin and Nod...
because the body is not done with them.

4.

From a Physics convention
in a city of one-room schoolhouses
and undergrounds. The keynote speaker

knew one word:
kinetic kinetic kinetic kinetic.

5.

To dusk at dawn. The longest escalator in the world
takes us down down down—
past the turnstiles, beside the leap
to the high voltage tracks,
to a hundred white moons blinking.

6.

Where a bookkeeper looks like T
before the goatee.
The library was full of old shoes.
I am told to search for a child's sandal
that fell from the L.

7.

To the moonfaced Madonna from the fourteenth century
in the west wing of the National Gallery.
She has just confessed to me
her suspended hand, pale and bored with perfection
in the twenty-first century
is going to reach down
to feel the child's genitals in her lap.

Song of the Nesting Doll

many are we one within the other
identical veils and sea roses on the sand
more than faces under transparent
shawls nimbus of bay-lit water shimmering
coastal afternoons when we were more than
forty-one less than six

do we end beginning
with a blue veil bigger than you and you
within the split torso
and you with the sleeves and rings nesting
eyes watching whales rise

undulating the surface dark
then gone back
under a nimbus kiss
what is within like

under the scent of night shade
twenty-seven back then
to reach all our selves we break

in the middle or twist shut
a long spring unguarded we

open

and open into
summer the widest place in the belly

a smaller me keeps spilling forth
and opening into a smaller me keeps
spilling forth and opening

what is it like without the nest
without containment beginning
or ending with wood sand shawl
least or most a voice too small for a face

our smallest mouth is but a red dot
can't open a dot too tiny to kiss
a sleeve disappearing on a wave
mute seed for a blue head
no hand to hold the cup

would you sing back to us
if you could open
with a voice all your own
would you speak more than and less
to us your chorus of sisters
your breasts of snow and shadow

White Road with Swan

I drove the back road because I wanted to see the swans in the snow.
  Snow
had fallen in the night, a light dusting easier to sweep than shovel.
It felt like a gift sent from someplace else,
intended for just this windless morning.

There were two swans, most likely a mated couple. I had seen them
  all winter,
drifting on the human pond or twisting their long necks to clean,
or dozing on their own hammocks of brown-gray water
in the lull of an afternoon.

At times I found them neck down, heads submerged into the
  stagnant water,
feeding or avoiding one another. I liked watching the limber of their
  long
necks, the wide wings they preened but never used. The swans
became less delicate, less white the more I watched.
I could not tell the male from female.

The white road reminded me of Helen whose name goes back to
  the child
of a woman and a god disguised as a swan. Helen who lost her mate
last summer. When she told me of the heart attack, she said he was
working in the garden, doing what he loved. Helen who is not
swan alone but also bear. And once I saw a snowy
owl fly into her, and then back out.

Driving the white road slowly to the swans that morning felt like my
  long ago.
I was good but could not do what was asked of me. The rattle of
  chains,

the scrunch of dry snow under wheels, anticipating the blow
of snow, the wind, the gates ajar of January.

I came to their curve but could not find them. I searched the gentle
    mallards
in their places. As if the dull pond were breathing, a mist rose where
the swans had ridden the winter. I searched the crusted sedge.
Maybe the swans thought this world was white enough
now a touch of snow had fallen.

Snowstorm

Be my ever desire
To be closed in by whiteness.
Let's play purity and belly the moon.

In the ceiling weather and mice
Carry on—ever so ever so.
The snow burns everything blind.

Could the snow run off with the flake?
Could the I run off with the eye?
Happily ever after would be we.

Together we'd listen to the punctuations of sky.
Snowflakes, lilacs, *do* spill. Hah!
Hills, hulls, lullabies.
Wind's longing for bones—imagine.
Snow without storm is all lull.

Together let's leap and picture summer.
Leaves listening to one another and smiling.
Nights on the altar of scent, sent home.
Afternoons with eardrums and animals but no sounds…
No that's more like snow.

The lightning bug is not trying to get our attention.
We'd follow her green lantern anywhere.
Into lightning,
Into aurora borealis,
Into the last great sentence of her.

And the *shiny Schultz*, the *dirty Duncan*—
Depending on whether it comes out

Inside out —
Is a masterpiece of logic.
Little wonder

The tribal women bury it,
The animal ingests it.
How like God is the mother
For a time and a half.

The soul has no I.
The soil has no I.
But soul and soil do have eyes.

Like snow.
Settling on our eye sockets.
Beginning to see us whole.

If it were up to me, we wouldn't leave the tail behind.
Go ahead and laugh at the imagination!
How our mouths are filling with snow.

Have we lost each other in the white where we began?

The Laurel

Membrane of leaf-mold wrapped round

                                                  her cranium

a fear fetal in the brain

                     leaf-heart green and kicking

damp earthen crown

                        harp sound of old wild flight

her hair flies out

                                whistles absolve

flows back

                        follicles chased / chaste

foliage falling over the god's

                            unbidden grasp

feet winged but not swift enough

                              of ground

her bare soles understand

                            sod rock craft and

grubbing worm made of

                     how far below the surface she

must reach

                                still running

toward air light breath

                                    yet rooted

rooted divinely in how dark

                                and purposeful

What Death Is Keeps Changing

Now it was the moon
circling the house.
The last week
of the millennium.

It was an unbidden smell,
incontinence, antiseptic
in the house, an impasse.

The bald eagles swooped
on every edge,
an old man's teeth
chattered from a chill.

His last words
eager for oxygen
began their flight,
winged from his bluish lips.

It was an exodus
no one living could track
or translate.

We fed him aspirin and humor
and heaped on quilts.
Whispered goodnight as if it were.

He called me the name
of his other daughter.

I caught that tenderness,
but how swift

it melted on my tongue,
one snowflake
robbed of winter.

Her name,
the last thing
he said to me.

Now it was crossing
the snow not far off.
Neither elk nor eagle turned
toward our vigil.

It was nothing
belonging to us.

The rest came through
a pale slope, like a dream's
sputtering energy, urgent
but useless when pulled
out of its own avalanche

girlfriend, fourteen, pork chops

A red light flared an hour
at the corner
without sound.
Another accident
outside the mind.

One more white dawn
the moon cracked open.

I listened for the sludge
of sorry but every stray
word had fled.

Now it was no longer
important.
A hushed wash
returned him
then took him farther out.

Now it was equable
pure breathing,
a transit soul.

From somewhere I heard
trust it   trust it

the body cast,
emptied of voice,
knows what to do
to stay itself
husk sack of fluids
breathwork
afterbirth
glutenous pulses all

stilling

Song for the Owl and Blind Man

for his drum at the root of dusk
for his heart in my gut
for his alert above the rock
for his eyes as mine shut

Who knows the night as well as he?

for the hills to which he hums
for the fright in the silent meadow
for wings predatory and sparing
for hands groping the cold logs

Who knows the night as well as he?

for hunger, burrow and soar
for home, salt and zinc
for the liver by dark, fur and bones
for earth by dawn

Who knows the night as well as he?

Overheard in an Orchard

The woman holding
the apple to her cheek
whispering

thankyou thankyou
you saved my life
my little brave one

the whole round O
scolded from you
but not gone

dwarf in the seed core
half in the earth
our work not done

you my sun-darkened bridge
my chasm healer child
me

I held the apple to my cheek
to my tongue
apple prayer

you had a voice all along
I heard a voice saying
I am only your resistance

make use of my sweetness
making hardly a sound
it was the whole orchard

thousands of loose vowels
falling earthward
scattering filling the air

snowfall and windshake
of white
blossom

The College's Copy of The Bell Jar

(with eight previously unpublished drawings)

Like common summer moth to flame I am drawn
into the story of Esther and Sylvia of Sylvia and Ted
the story of the Tedless Sylvia of Sylvia and mother Aurelia
the episode of Esther without her mother Mrs. Greenwood
and the family root cellar Dr. Nolan and the mother's visits
the episode of the burned sequel manuscript the birthday
present enflamed in the pyre of Sylvia furious without Ted
the missing journals as told by the Sylviafamous Ted
and the EstherSylvia guest editorship at *Mademoiselle*
the pinnacles and the chasms the medicine cabinet key
the crawl space that smelled like the sea the discovery
the slow recovery the electroshock therapy psychotherapy
letters and partial journals the morning oven and the drained
face that left two glasses of milk beside the sleeping
children in a room strategically taped to keep carbon
monoxide out the concerned neighbor knocked
unconscious in the downstairs flat the more or less complete
typed manuscript that survived the gas the old loves the eight
previously unpublished drawings to which I'm as drawn
as to another reader's thick pink highlighter on page eight
snaking through *like a secret voice*
speaking straight out of my own bones and joining the
stubby pink "ALTER EGO" trying to make the leap
after *bones* followed by the messy possibly intoxicated
same pink squiggle "White Heaven Like" on page 52
in vast contrast to the tidiest little vertical "eating disorder"
poised in black pen on 174 with its prim perfect arrow
pointing to the passage where Esther buries her hotdog
in the sand when nobody is looking prefaced by
the same austere black arrow appearing on page 170
where it abuts *I fingered the box of razors*

in my pocketbook before which on page 96
a Greek chorus of penciled stars gathers round
I grew gloomier and gloomier and returns on page 142
to swarm *I hadn't washed my hair for three weeks*
I hadn't slept for seven nights and comes back for
a grand finale a bursting of penciled stars like the best
and last of the fireworks surrounding two whole sentences
on 185 where Esther contemplates converting to Catholicism
since Catholics consider killing oneself a deadly sin such that
I have started to question the unabashed "what's gone wrong?"
penciled in the margin beside the paragraph on 148 where
Esther Greenwood also considers moving to Chicago and
changing her name to Elly Higginbottom can't this dear reader
tell what's gone wrong by page 148 although I cannot tell
whether it is the same led pencil drawn like a coffin around
the word *hearse* on page 163 along with its attendant arrow
to "death!" hurried in decisive cursive and hovering
in the outer margin like an excited angel but I am positive
it is the same steadfast pink reader who is drinking her way
through the bell jar and making a flamboyant pink
highway through page 139's *I hated the very idea*
of the eighteenth century, with all those smug men
writing tight little couplets and being so dead
keen on reason even as I question why she did not
highlight and brighten the tight little black and white scrim
drawings after the story ends: the rubber tire the wooden
tool chest cast iron stove dress shoes thatched cottage
the fishing boats on one of those stormy
inscrutable sea days roped snug to the grim piers.

Accomplishment

We sleep while the day begins again
                              its own private lists in the sloppy dark.
The dark is an arsenal of the disembodied—
stampede, ammunition, kerosene, tongue
bitten off by its own terror.

A woman in broken English breaks in to say: *Generators?*
We are a poor country... People here live on $20 a month...
                              We cannot afford generators to...
voice cut off in that combustible style of journalistic diplomacy.

The fog persists this day I cannot see the hill
                              nor the winter slash pile afire.
Even at noon our day is a bowl of nightfall,
                              a long greenish shiver of thick dusk,
one giant shadowing another.

Now we occupy an old city breathing between ancient rivers.
Chaos of the populace in the dirt streets, another victory
                              accomplished for our arrogance
                                                  our failure.

Failure

Another failed accomplishment for our arrogant old.
                Streets of chaos, populace in the ancient dirt
rivering between breath and city.
                      We shadow now another occupation,
giant shivering one, dusk of long greenish nightfall,
bowl even the thick noonday afire is after.

               Nor the slash,
the hill pile I cannot winter,
                cannot persist the fog of diplomacy this day
cut off in journalistic voice, that style combustible.

Country, we are a poor generator,
                   cannot we people a woman broken
in English generators to live here, to afford to say $20 breaks in on
its own bitten-off month by a terror…?

Tongue, kerosene, ammunition, stampede,
                   disembodied arsenal of the dark,
its own sloppy lists are darkly private
         while our sleep begins the day again.

Joy

The day you left
the sky wept
six days the mountain hid
bobcat bear deer coyote rabbit
bloated from the sudden upland puddles

part of you stayed behind
to love the mud back
your palm prints
softened with
hoof tongue paw

with old thirst and red earth
earth made clay by rain
you were not done
banks of the filled arroyos
felt your feet

patter the washed-out path
handfuls of snails fell
into the empty garden
rain fattened the apricots
a flat roof dripped

you pulled from the owl
apologies for the lost cats
the river pushed and gushed
the mesas slicked past all darks
the desert shivered

would not shine whole
no thing
nothing
not changed
by your going.

The Desert Where You Began

That first desert you will not remember.
No word for blue, for the underside
of the lizard scurrying back to brown.
Like the desert you made no sound.
Small mouth at breast, dangling feet
that lost the thumb-sized socks.
We crossed the rattlesnake still calm
on the morning path's volcano shadow.

—*all you come from*—I heard the desert think
so turned the intricate cradle of your ears
into it—virga, lava, sandstone, tail—
I walked its dry sounds into your skin,
I rocked the old rock back in,
into your forming bones.

Desert Grace

Let this city become a dim adobe room
where I will not sleep again. Let sun *sol*
and moon *luna* mind the rock
mountain I have clung to for seven years.
I never chose this desert, this mountain.
I landed here one winter solstice
after a flight too dark for thought.
I awoke to its searing light,
its watery, vivid languages. Hungry
and ready, I claimed arroyos and
riverbed, bosques and mesas,
cottonwoods and cloudless sky.
I walked its spine convinced it was mine.
I was like the phoenix, I let the desert
burn me into another form.

Watermelon. A difficult fruit to grow
in a parched place. Those explorers
who rode north on horseback searching
for the seven cities must have met
this mountain afire at dusk
and been blinded. Out of thirst
they named the reddish peaks
Sandias, an elemental melon.
They slashed this desert with
names and seeds, guns and crucifixes,
orchards and problematic missions.
They never found the gold
they came looking for. Nor did I.
Instead I found an underworld
filled with sunlight.
Scrape of knees and elbows,
rock and bone. I discovered

shadow is made of gold,
desert a body made sacred
by danger and wound.

If just once I would belong to a place
as song before my leaving,
I would ask to be the tremolo
in the "Amazing Grace" I heard
a small schoolgirl sing alone
one evening on the sandy playground.
Her voice was like the sun's brief
and nightly serenade to the *Sandias*,
imperfect in its passion,
older than her seven years, older than
the cities sprawled out under her feet,
not yet lost, not yet wounded
and still soft, floating and aglow
against the falling dark.

Santuario

I would be your soft brown shadow on the mud wall cast
by the weathered gate pushed open or the wooden door
the round courtyard with crosses risen from dust
any pigeon bobbing in juniper shade for berries crumbs
seeds the twin bell towers I would volunteer my only voice
to form your twelve vertical peals at noon that startle
reenact restore my hands and feet to keep the dry geometry
between plank bench and adobe wall both sides your tourist
and native your pilgrim and resident priest twigs crossed
in the fence your every morning earth miraculous
the anteroom stacked with crutches but you said *no*
you will belong to no place no shadow of a threshold
that is your answer your pilgrimage
your dust that is not your tongue

Avocado

Awe
begins in
the avocado when
it's soft but not overly
overtly soft soft green but not
bruised or brown ah that kind
of avocado selling five for a dollar
in the corner markets in San
Francisco San Diego pesos
for avocados in Mexico and south
south a soft voice singing
from a yellow window
a bird a girl her avocado lull
her sweetness kept safely avocado
in tough unscented skin oh
the avocado's love is an oval
seed afloat in a rich green boat
and a cello a yellow avocado cello
with its low o sound like skin touched
in favor of skin yes there should be
ah in the beginning and
oh in the end—full round sounds
the off-centered oddity of the pit
encasing the slippery truth of sprout
and between the end and the beginning
there's guacamole—a whole life
a dance tossed loosely in a gold bowl
and a daughter's name in the most
palatable avocado Ah-va
bird and life and an ode
an ocarina to echo the bold
avocado cello.

Ocarina cello and voice
a three-tiered cord—birth cord
brown unseen seed green flesh
a daughter's strong song.
What's in an avocado?—Ah!
the vocation
the vocalization of
awe!

To the Flowering Dogwood

Time would never force us to love your white umbrella lace
your rain beside the April road your initial grace

spring deepened our house so missing the absent festival
death sprung some distance to guard your spacious grace

time carved the mind of our April son who was two
ran nude and learned to climb within your gnarled grace

he blossomed beside the old dog guarding the festival
of nests the white road umbrellaed by your falling grace

time loved the absentminded ones who so missed their house
(ours now) forced into oldness under your three Graces

running nude and nesting in our son who was ten
one spring carving initials into your leaning grace

time climbed the wood the dog fell deep some distance laced
with death blossom to reign beneath your explosive grace

Molt

This is my way of wanting the trees to teach me
the grace of loss the *duende* of failure
the simultaneity of green and groan
           let go and belong

white pines I cannot spread a blanket large enough
to gather all that is dropping out of the woodsy sky
feathers pine needles leaves skin I cannot
lie beneath without hearing the sigh rise again
the sunken cheek the whisker hair still growing
fathoming
           corpse and egg

the snake skin dangles over my head
in wind it sways against the trunk
it shimmers empty as a wing

haven't I too chosen routes that dead end
haven't I vanished and come back into my own bones
walking or winding or whispering
           over and under you

Visitant

Here you are again arriving
in your vast American sedan
crossing a western field a wind clean
space to visit as if you were
designated your wheels imprinting
the vulnerable ground
making your own
road back

why have you come I know
you will not answer years
have passed since you began
your leaving you look so healthy
your hair

has grown back even though
you still wear the straw fishing
hat too small for your head
you have gained some weight
and look quite fit for a man your age
though you remind me
age does not matter
our time

is so brief in the body
I run to greet you
open my arms rest my ear
near your gut hear it gurgle
and we breathe in sync
even as I begin the morning
asking who are you for me

now that you
are gone

Ten Seconds in Early Spring

A boy passed out in Health Class on the first day of First Aid.
In a month he would turn thirteen. He could feel the oblivion
coming quickly without warning, without voice or name.

His eyes spotted a blurry movement. Was it a soldier or
bear groggy from winter foraging at the edge of dark pines?
He blinked and could no longer trust his eyes.

He saw his wonderful life fleeing somewhere without him,
shadowing into the forest like a child running too fast
to keep up with, his belly and his working blood

filling with dizzies, a bright coiling in his tummy like the
snakes one learns to avoid, the red swift drain of color,
strange but beautiful dangers, the loss of control, primal

locus of pain. His teacher had just begun the lesson,
was announcing the topics: vomiting, seizures, types of wounds,
symptoms of shock, fainting, and what to do about bleeding.

The words *blood* and *wound* pulled him under. His eyes closed
like a bright machine that seizes and suddenly stops. Meanwhile,
out in the woods the delicate bloodroot were

rupturing the spongy earth, bearing its tang to return.
A season can manage that much change in increments of seconds.
But I don't believe a boy can. Ashen he fell away

from his desk, a black gravity twisting him down
to cold ground. An elbow bruised, a cheek chafed
and swelled. Blood broke from the skin of his forehead.

He saw, felt, none of this. Later, he would learn
it took all of ten seconds on his wristwatch:
five seconds of falling, five of being fallen.

When he came to, he recognized voices, the hard
classroom floor where his arms shivered. At first,
he did not open his eyes, did not speak.

Although he knew he was not crying,
he could feel his cheeks drenched
by that child who had left him abruptly

and weeping.

After Winter

I go out walking and cross old catastrophes on the ground,
    tufts of loose fur, a splay of drab feathers,
        a scatter of snow-soaked bones,
            no evidence of blood or struggle.

I find shells dropped a great height from the pines,
    a whole blue egg at my feet,
        a white turtle egg impervious as rubber,
        a broken limb, vague war.

It no longer feels like enough to praise the morning,
    to marvel at the promise of eggs.
        All winter I wanted someone to lead me more than me,
          I wanted a whole person to preside, to bow his head.

From the ground and air I hear attack and scold,
    attack and scold. Crows and dogs, grackles and jays.
        Even mild robins squabble over
        one thin worm, half in, half out

of its small black tunnel the color of oil, the worm
    fighting back to do the one thing it can,
        to keep death alive.
            I'll still love my country, this thawing puzzle of soil,

        I'll still risk trust,
            white slope of the child everlasting,
            incremental,
                turning underfoot to green.

Notes

"Togwotee" refers to a mountainous region in northwestern Wyoming where the Continental Divide forms the headwaters of both Atlantic and Pacific drainages. The word is of Shoshone origin, and locals know it to mean "you can go anywhere from here."

"Snowstorm" is partially a "found poem." Many of its phrases came from Post-it notes on Sandra Kray's copy of *The Night Path*, where her grandmother Bam had scribbled personal responses.

All italicized phrases in the poem, "The College's Copy of *The Bell Jar*," are from *The Bell Jar*, Sylvia Plath, Harper & Row, 1971.

Acknowledgments

Grateful acknowledgment is made to the editors of the following journals and anthologies, in which these poems first appeared, sometimes in slightly different forms:

American Journal of Nursing: "April Nights," "Song for the Coming of
    Winter";
Journal of Mythic Arts (online): "The Voice Outside";
Kestrel: "The First Time I Saw My Father Cry," "Under the Risings";
Orion: "Molt";
The Southern Review: "Mount Zion Road";
Spiritus: "Skin."

"Clothesline" appeared in *Sweeping Beauty: Contemporary Women Poets on Housework*, edited by Pamela Gemin.

A book that grows as slowly as this did owes thanks to many people in many places; for those who remain unnamed, I hope you will recognize your good influences. I gratefully acknowledge James Madison University for a year's leave that gave me continuous time; the Virginia Commission for the Arts for a Literary Fellowship; my students in Virginia and New Mexico for teaching me so much; my husband, Kevin, who built not one but two writing spaces; my children, Weston and Ava, who watched me come and go from them. I thank Peg Cronin and Rita Gabis for living so closely with so many poems; Thom Ward and Peter Conners at BOA, for their insightful Post-it notes and strong hunches; Jeanie Tomanek for permission to use her art. Special thanks to Andrea Hollander Budy and Joy Jacobson who took on the first unruly draft and did not back away.

Many poems in this book are in memory of Leo V. Love, my friend; G.L. Kutchins, my father; Stanley Kunitz and Ralph Ziegler, my elders.

About the Author

Laurie Kutchins is the author of *Between Towns* (Texas Tech University Press) and *The Night Path*, which received the inaugural Isabella Gardner Poetry Award from BOA Editions, Ltd. in 1997. Her poems and nonfiction have appeared widely in journals and anthologies, including *The Georgia Review*, *The New Yorker*, *Ploughshares*, *The Kenyon Review*, *LIT*, and *The Southern Review*. She teaches in the creative writing program at James Madison University in the Shenandoah Valley of Virginia, at the Taos Summer Writers Conference, and summers along the Wyoming-Idaho border.

BOA Editions, Ltd.
American Poets Continuum Series

Colophon

Slope of the Child Everlasting, poems by Laurie Kutchins, is set in Monotype Dante with Corsiva used for display. Dante was first created in metal type in the mid-1950s and digitalized in the 1990s, the result of a collaboration between Giovanni Mardersteig—a printer, book designer, and typeface artist renowned for the work he produced at Officina Bodoni and Stamperia Valdònega in Italy—and Charles Malin, one of the great punch-cutters of the twentieth century. Monotype Corsiva is an italic typeface made in the style of the early Italian cursives as exemplified by the work of the writing master Ludovico degli Arrighi in the sixteenth century.

The publication of this book was made possible, in part, by the special support of the following individuals:

Anonymous (6)
Nancy & Alan Cameros
Craig Challender
Gwen & Gary Conners
Margaret E. Cronin   •   Susan DeWitt Davie
Peter & Sue Durant
Pete & Bev French
Dane & Judy Gordon
Kip & Deb Hale
Robin & Peter Hursh
Richard & Catherine Massie
Stanley D. McKenzie
Boo Poulin
Deborah Ronnen
Thomas R. Ward in memory of Jane Buell Ward
Mike & Pat Wilder
Glenn & Helen William

CPSIA information can be obtained
at www.ICGtesting.com
Printed in the USA
FSHW021045200619
59256FS